1. Color circles with a marker.

2. Attach wiggle eyes.

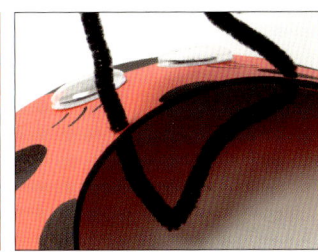
3. Attach chenille stems.

Ladybug

Clever and cute, this Ladybug will complete your look.

SIZE: 4" wide brim
MATERIALS: Red foam visor • Black foam marker • 1 Black chenille stem • 2 wiggle eyes 30mm • 1/8" hole punch • Foam adhesive
INSTRUCTIONS: Using a Black marker, outline visor edge, and draw random circles. Glue wiggle eyes in place. Draw eyelashes above eyes. Punch 2 holes for antennae into top rim of visor 2½" apart. Bend chenille stem into a "U", poke both ends through holes from back to front, swirl antenna ends with your fingers.

Green Caterpillar

This bright visor is easy to make!

SIZE: 4" wide brim
MATERIALS: Green foam visor • Foam (Green pom-poms, Sticky Sheets (Red, Green, Light Green) • Green marker • Chenille stems (3 Lime Green, Red) • 2 eyes 20 mm • 1/8" hole punch • Glitter glue • Adhesive
INSTRUCTIONS: Cut sticky sheets into ½" wide strips: 3 Green, 2 Light Green, 2 Red. Trim to size and adhere to visor. • Cut chenille stems to match each strip and adhere in place. Add a wavy line of glitter glue to foam strips. Let dry. • Glue eyes onto visor. Draw eye details below eyes. • Punch 2 holes for antennae 2" apart in the center of visor top rim. Bend Green chenille stem into a "U", poke both ends through holes from back to front. Poke Green foamie pompom onto end of chenille stick and bend into loose swirl with your fingers.

1. Add a wavy line of glitter glue to the foam strip.

2. Add pompom to stem.

Daffodils Visor

Fabulous and fun... this visor is great fun to make.

SIZE: 4" wide brim
MATERIALS: White foam visor • Yellow daffodil 1½" diameter silk flowers • White mini brads • Push pin
INSTRUCTIONS:
Using push pin, poke 15 holes evenly across the top rim of visor. • Attach each silk flower with a brad.

1. Poke holes with a push pin.

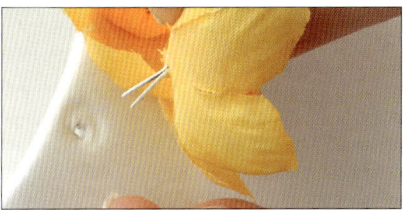
2. Attach flowers with brads.

3. Push brad open.

Foam and Glitter 3

Card with Flowers

This card is the perfect complement for the Flower bracelet.

SIZE: 4¼" x 5"

MATERIALS:
18 foam flowers ⅜" to 1" • 5" x 8½" White cardstock • 4" x 5" striped paper • 9 White minibrads • Rub-on words "There is no one like you" • *Clearsnap* Blue Lagoon Chalk ink • Push pin

INSTRUCTIONS:
Fold cardstock in half. • Cover front with striped paper. Cut an uneven wave along front of card. Ink all card edges. • Poke holes ½" apart along the bottom of card front. Layer foam flowers varying size and color and attach to card with mini brads. Add rub-on words.

Flower Bracelet

Soft, pretty, and fun to wear, every little girl is going to want one of these Flower bracelets.

SIZE: 8"

MATERIALS:
Foam flowers ⅜" to 1" • Stretchy cord 1.0 • 8mm and 6mm bicone beads (Pink, Orange)

INSTRUCTIONS:
Measure wrist, add 2" for tying off. • Tie 1 end of stretchy cord. String 1 bead, 4 flowers, 1 bead, 4 flowers. Repeat until the cord is full. Tie ends securely. Trim ends.

1. Stack sequin and flower. Attach to letter with a pin.

Flowered "A"

Initials are a hot decorating item. The Flowered Letter is a fun activity for any party.

SIZE: 5" x 5" x 1"

MATERIALS:
Foam (Letter, Flowers ⅜" to 1") • ¾" ball head straight pins • Neon color sequins

INSTRUCTIONS:
Pair a foam flower with a sequin. Pin into foam. Cover foam letter with flowers.

Pansy Flower

This is also a fun project to do with the Scouts for Mother's Day.

SIZE: 4½" x 7"

MATERIALS:
Lavender foam flower shape • Green sticky foam sheet • Chenille stems (Lime Green, Purple) • 8 small pompoms • Push pin • Wire cutters • Foam adhesive

INSTRUCTIONS:
Trace flower leaves and stem onto back of Green sticky sheet. Cut out. Stick onto flower form covering Lavender leaves and stem. Cut Purple chenille stems into five 4½" pieces. Bend a right angle in the last ¼" of each end. Form a flower petal. Poke 2 holes towards the middle of each flower petal with a push pin. Thread ends of Purple stem into holes and press down on back of flower. Repeat for each petal. Cut 2 Green chenille stems 6" long. Apply to leaves as with petals. Glue Yellow pompoms to the center of flower.

1. Bend a right angle into the ends of the chenille stem.

2. Push bent ends into holes in the foam.

3. Glue pompoms to center.

Notes Message Board

Everyone will notice your important message when written on this fun Notes Message Board.

SIZE: 7½" x 10½"
MATERIALS:
Dry Erase Foam Flower Board with marker • Foam sticky sheets (Green, Purple) • 3 foam flowers ¾" • 6mm pompoms • Foam paint (White, Purple, Lime) • Foam adhesive
INSTRUCTIONS:
Board: Dip a small pompom in White paint and dab dots onto foam flower board randomly. Let dry. Add a Purple paint dot to the center of each White dot. Let dry. Run a bead of adhesive around marker board and add pompoms. • Cut leaf from Green sticky sheet using pattern. Write the word "Notes" onto Leaf in White, adding details in Lime foam paint. Let dry. Adhere leaf to flower board back.
Pen: Cut a ½" strip of Purple sticky foam, peel and wrap diagonally around marker. Trim ends to fit. Adhere 3 flowers to covered pen.

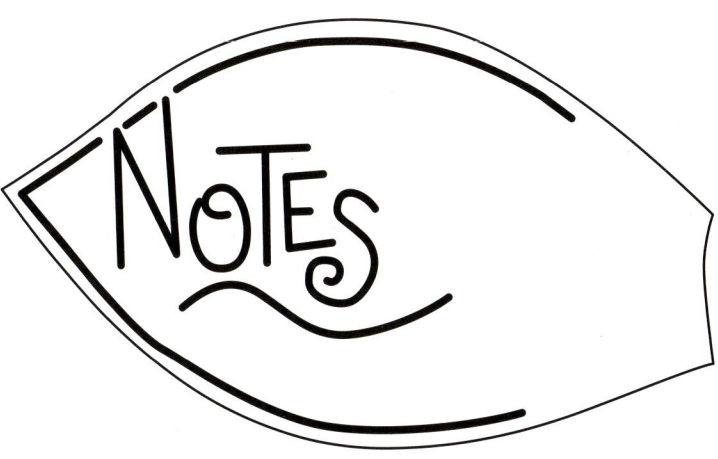

1. Add details with foam paint.

2. Wrap marker with a foam strip.

Pen Holder

Make a holder or drink coozie that is pretty for a princess.

SIZE: 3½" diameter, 4" tall
MATERIALS:
Purple foam coozie • 6 sticky castles • 22 gauge non-tarnish Silver wire • Plastic bead assortment (Purple, Pink) • Push pin • Wire cutter • Round-nose pliers
INSTRUCTIONS:
Poke holes evenly around top of coozie. • Cut 24" of wire. In one end, turn a loop and a small swirl. Thread through first hole from the inside to the outside, add 4-5 beads, insert through next hole from inside to outside. Repeat all around coozie. Finish off with a loop and small swirl to secure wire. Add castles to bottom of coozie, trimming as needed to fit.

Cupcake Marker

SIZE: 1½" x 2"
MATERIALS:
Foam Lavender sticky sheet • *Sizzix* die cut machine & star die • Purple rhinestones • Tinsel • Toothpicks • Black foam marker • Opal glitter glue
INSTRUCTIONS:
Die cut 2 stars for each wand marker. Write name of "princess" on 1 star, and paint with Opal glitter glue. Let dry. • Peel backing off stars and sandwich toothpick and a small amount of tinsel between stars. Adhere a Purple rhinestone.

Foam and Glitter 5

1. Adhere cut pieces to cross.

Mosaic John 3:16 Cross

Create a message of love with this simple mosaic technique.

SIZE: 7" x 9½"

MATERIALS:
Red Cross Foamie magnetic shape • Foam Sticky sheets (Red, White, Navy, Purple, Lavender)

INSTRUCTIONS:
Cut out Red heart using pattern. Cut into random bits and piece back together onto cross. • Cut Navy, Purple, and Lavender foam into small pieces. Cover cross with random mosaic. Cut letters from White foam and stick in place. • Trim away pieces that overlap the edge of cross.

Princess Scrapbook Page

Foam is safe and acid free for your scrapbook projects. Incorporate this beautiful dimensional technique into your pages just for fun.

SIZE: 7" x 7"

MATERIALS:
Foam sticky sheet (2½" x 7" Purple, 2" x 2" Green) • Sticky foam flowers (Purple, White) • ½" Purple sparkle foam letters • 12" x 12" double-sided Green cardstock • Purple 8mm rhinestones • Opal glitter glue • Foam adhesive

INSTRUCTIONS:
Cut cardstock 8" x 8" and 4" x 6". Cut pieces from Purple foam strip to form a mosaic border, keeping pieces in order as you cut. Apply to 8" cardstock as a border on left side of page. • Using other side of cardstock, adhere mat and photo next to border, leaving room for "princess" title at the top. Cut leaves from Green sticky foam. Peel and stick leaves and flowers to embellish page. Glue rhinestones to flower centers. Add additional detail to flowers with Opal glitter glue. Let dry. Apply "princess" stickers above photo.

Pink Journal

Personalize a journal for yourself or make one as a gift for a friend.

SIZE: 6" x 8"
MATERIALS:
6" x 8" Pink foam journal • 4½" x 6½" White foam sticky sheet • 8 foam flowers ⅜" to 1" • ½" foam letters • 4 White minibrads • Pink glitter glue • 20" Pink ⅝ ribbon cut into five 4" pieces • Push pins
INSTRUCTIONS:
Adhere White foam sheet to book front. Trace edge of White foam with glitter glue. Let dry. • Poke a hole in 2 corners of White foam, also piercing book. Layer foam flowers and attach with mini brads. Attach other flowers. Apply sticky letters. Tie ribbon pieces onto journal spiral.

All Tied Up Visor

Express your personal style with ribbons to match your favorite summer outfit.

SIZE: 4" wide brim
MATERIALS:
Pink foam visor • 4" strips ⅝" Black ribbon (8 Black gingham, 9 Black with flowers) • ¼" hole punch
INSTRUCTIONS:
Punch holes at ½" intervals around top rim of visor. Feed alternating ribbons through each hole and tie in a knot.

1. Tie a ribbon in each hole.

1. Outline around flowers and fill in flower centers with glitter glue.

Flower Visor

Sweet and sparkling, the Flower Frenzy visor makes a bold fashion statement.

SIZE: 4" wide brim
MATERIALS:
Black foam visor • 3 each foam 1½" flowers (Pink, Purple, White) • Lavender glitter glue
INSTRUCTIONS:
Stick flowers on visor. Add Lavender glitter glue to flower centers. Let dry. Draw outline around flowers with Lavender glitter glue. Let dry.

Foam and Glitter 7

1. Stamp flowers randomly onto foam sheet.

2. Accent letters with a Black foam marker.

Let's Party

Get the party started with fun decorations. No girl would miss this party!

SIZE: Invitation 4½" x 8½", Seat marker 3¼" x 4¾", Frame 6" x 8"

MATERIALS:
Sticky foam sheet (8" x 11" Pink, 3" x 3" White, 2 Teal 1" circles) • 4" x 6" Pink-Teal magnetic foam frame • Pink foam ¾" letters • *Plaid* foam flower block stamp • 2 small and 2 large each sticky flowers (Pink, White) • 10 Teal 9mm rhinestones • 3 each ribbons 8" long (Pink, White, Striped) • Rub-on letters • 8" x 11" White cardstock • Black foam marker • Fuchsia craft paint • Crop-A-Dile punch • Sponge brush • Foam adhesive

INSTRUCTIONS:

Prep: Apply Fuchsia paint to foam flower stamp with a sponge brush. Stamp randomly over Pink foam sheet and foam letter. Let dry.

Invitation: Cut out 2 tag shapes 4½" x 8½". Cut remaining flowers from leftover foam. Print or write invitation details on cardstock. Peel backing from Pink tags and apply to back of printed cardstock, carefully lining up words with tag. Trim cardstock to fit tag. Repeat for each tag. Adhere cut out stamped foam flowers inside as desired. • Place tags together, with Teal circles at point. Punch holes through the circles and tags. Tie with ribbons. Sandwich each ribbon end between 2 flowers. • Adhere White square on cover, draw Black dotted line with foam marker, and adhere foam letters. Glue rhinestones to flower centers as desired.

"J" Seat Marker: Apply rub-on letters to name each person attending the party. Glue Teal rhinestones to flower centers as desired.

Frame: Apply Fuchsia paint to foam flower stamp with a sponge brush. Stamp randomly over frame. Let dry. Glue Teal rhinestones in the middle of whole flowers. Insert a favorite party photo.

Crown

Crown your princess with a personalized flowered tiara.

SIZE: 4" brim
MATERIALS:
Pink foam tiara • 10 foam flowers ⅜" to 1" • ½" foam sticky letters • 5 White mini brads • Push pin
INSTRUCTIONS:
Poke holes across top of tiara on points. Layer foam flowers varying size and color and attach to tiara with mini brads. Apply letters.

Star Wand

Complete a royal ensemble with a sparkling Star Wand.

SIZE: 4½" x 10½"
MATERIALS:
Pink foam 4½" star • 12" dowel rod ¼" diameter • 24" ribbon ¼" wide (Pink, White) • Pink acrylic paint • Silver glitter glue • Foam adhesive
INSTRUCTIONS:
Paint dowel Pink. Paint star with glitter glue. Let dry. • Poke dowel into the base of the star to make a hole. Apply foam adhesive to the tip of the dowel and insert into star. Let dry. Wrap ribbons around dowel at base of star.

'Knock Please' Door Hanger

"Knock, Please", there is a genius at work. Make a colorful door sign for everyone's room.

SIZE: 5" x 10½"
MATERIALS:
Pink flower foam door hanger • Pink silk hydrangea petals pulled from stem • Brads (Yellow, Pink) • *Making Memories* foam letter stamps • Raspberry craft paint • Black foam marker • Sponge brush • Push pin
INSTRUCTIONS:
Apply Raspberry paint to foam letters with sponge brush. Stamp on door hanger below flower. Let dry. • Outline letters and write "please" with Black foam marker. • Poke holes around inside of flower. Layer 2 flower heads together and attach with a brad.

1. Apply Raspberry paint to a stamp with a sponge brush.

2. Attach flowers to the door hanger with brads.

1. Swirl wire ends.

2. Sandwich stem between two leaves.

Tiny Flower Pot

Brighten someone's day with a pretty pot of flowers.
SIZE: 1½" x 3" tall
MATERIALS:
Sticky foam flowers, circles (Pink, Orange) • Yellow 1" foam swirl • Green ½" x 1" foam leaves • 2 Green chenille stems • 5 pieces Silver 22 gauge wire 3" long • 18" Green ¼" ribbon • Orange rhinestone • 1½" bottom diameter Silver bucket • Green decorative grass • Orange glitter glue • Green foam marker • Round-nose pliers • Foam adhesive
INSTRUCTIONS:
Sandwich chenille stems between matching foam flowers. Swirl wire ends with pliers. Sandwich wires under center circles. Add details with Orange glitter glue. Glue Orange rhinestone to center of one large flower. • Sandwich chenille stems with foam leaves. Also sandwich leaves around top of the bucket. Glue ribbon around top of bucket. • Cut stems at varying lengths, poke into foam block for stability, place in the bottom of bucket. Cover with decorative grass.

1. Knot 1 end. Push ribbon through first hole, thread 3 beads, knot.

2. Knot the end of ribbon, thread 3 beads, push through hole, add 3 beads, knot. Repeat.

3. Doodle around frame with Green Jelly Roll pen.

'Raftin' the River' Photo Keeper

Relive the fun! Display your fabulous vacation photos in a photo keeper that is as interesting as the event.
SIZE: 5" x 6½"
MATERIALS:
Yellow and Green 4" x 6" foam photo keeper • Foam bugs (3 Green, 2 Yellow) • Pony beads (11 Green, 11 Yellow, 11 Gold) • 6 Green ¼" wide ribbons 4" long • Green Jelly Roll pen • Crop-A-Dile punch
INSTRUCTIONS:
Punch 11 holes across bottom of keeper cover ½" apart. • Tie a knot in the end of 1 ribbon, add 3 beads, insert ribbon in first hole. Knot. • Ribbon 2: Knot the end, string 3 beads, thread down through second hole and up through third hole, add three beads, knot. • Repeat to complete beaded edge. Write words and doodle around frame with Green pen. • Stick a Green bug on the cover. Adhere bugs to individual pages to form tabs.

1. Apply rub-ons to frame.

Lime Fun Frame

Quick, easy, and fun, rub-ons provide endless possibilities for giving a frame its own unique style.

SIZE: 6" x 8"

MATERIALS:
Lime foam frame • Rub-on flowers • Sticky rhinestones (Blue, Green) • 28" Green ribbon ⅜" wide • Crop-A-Dile hole punch

INSTRUCTIONS:
Rub on flowers randomly. Add rhinestones. • Punch a hole in the top corners of the frame. Thread the ribbon through the holes and tie a bow for hanging.

1. Apply glitter glue details to dragonfly on the Caterpillar Frame.

Caterpillar Frame

Foam critters sparkle on this cute frame.

SIZE: 6" x 8"

MATERIALS:
Foam (4" x 6" Blue magnetic frame, White letters, Green caterpillar, Green-Blue dragonfly) • Glitter glue (Opal, Blue) • Foam markers (Black, Blue, White) • 4" Silver 22 gauge non-tarnish wire • Wire cutters • Round-nose pliers • Foam adhesive

INSTRUCTIONS:
Outline circles on caterpillar body with marker, alternating White and Blue. Draw a smile and antennas. Use glitter glue to accent the body. Glue caterpillar to frame. • Outline White letters with Blue marker and stick to frame. • Cut wire into two 2" pieces. Make antennae by turning a loop with round-nose pliers into each wire end, then swirling. Poke the other end directly into dragonfly head. Add details on dragonfly and stick to frame.

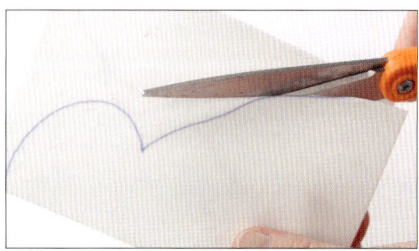
1. Draw shapes on foam. Cut out.

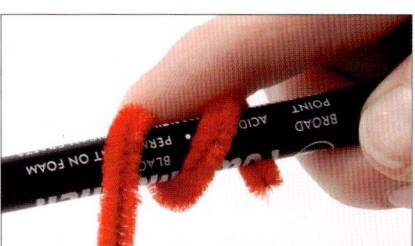
2. Curl chenille stem around marker.

3. Apply glitter glue to snowballs.

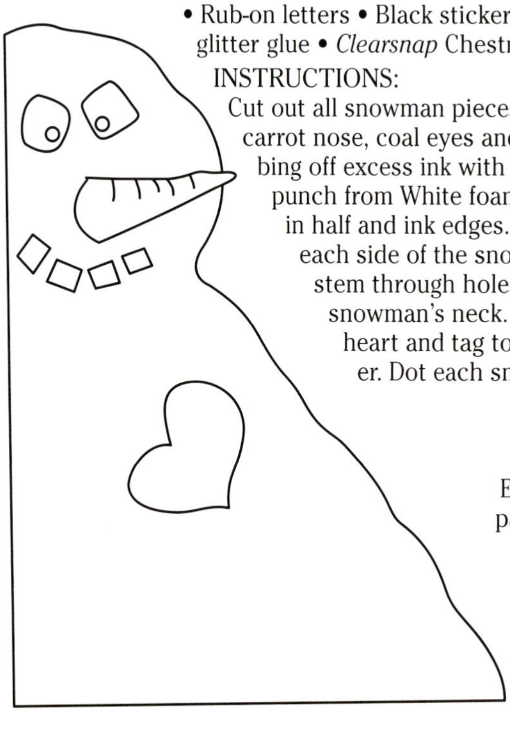

'Cold Hands, Warm Heart' Card

Melt someone's heart with a cheery greeting.

SIZE: 5¼" x 6¼"

MATERIALS:
Foam sticky sheets (White, Red, Black, Orange) • White foam letters (1" and ½") • 6½" x 11" Blue cardstock • 3" White organza ¼" wide ribbon • Red chenille stem • 1 small White tag • Rub-on letters • Black sticker letters • Foam markers (White, Black) • Opal glitter glue • *Clearsnap* Chestnut Roan chalk ink • Hole punch (¼", ⅛")

INSTRUCTIONS:
Cut out all snowman pieces and heart from foam using patterns. Adhere carrot nose, coal eyes and mouth. Ink snowman & heart edges, rubbing off excess ink with paper towel. • Punch 20 circles with each punch from White foam. Adhere all over snowman. • Fold cardstock in half and ink edges. Stick snowman on card. • Poke a hole on each side of the snowman's neck. Thread ends of Red chenille stem through holes from inside of card. Twist in place around snowman's neck. Curl ends around a marker. • Add words, heart and tag to card. Outline White letters with Black marker. Dot each snowball with Opal glitter glue. Let dry.

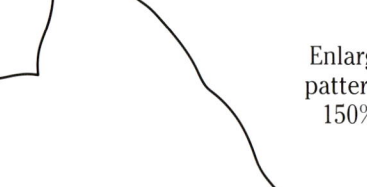

Enlarge patterns 150%

'Dillon's Room' Door Hanger

So clever! Dillon's door hanger has a different message on each side.

SIZE: 3¼" x 9½"

MATERIALS:
Black foam door hanger • ½" Blue foam letters • Sticky foam sheet (Red, Grey, White, Black, Yellow) • Glitter glue (Black, Opal)

INSTRUCTIONS:
Using patterns, cut out car parts from foam sheets. Stick one part on each side of the door hanger. Add tires. Adhere letters. Peel backing and stick windows, stripes and lightning onto car.
• Working 1 side at a time, apply glitter glue to tires, windows, numbers, and lightning. Let dry.

1. Adhere windows, lightning, and stripes to car.

1. Stamp soccer ball on White foam and cut out.

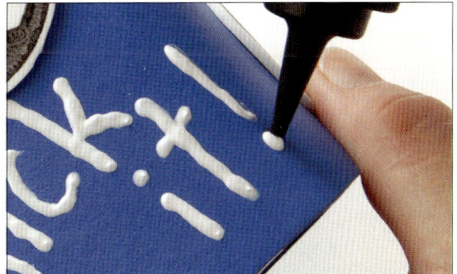

2. Add words with White foam paint.

'Soccer's the Sport!' Bottle Holder and Cupcake Marker

Kick off a great soccer season with a bottle coozie to please every fan. After the game, serve up these cupcakes with individually numbered markers.

SIZE: Coozie 3½" diameter, 4" tall; Cupcake marker 2" diameter, 3½" tall

MATERIALS:
Blue foam coozie • White sticky foam sheet • Red number rub-ons • 2 toothpicks • *Plaid* Soccer Ball foam stamp • Black craft paint • White foam paint • Sponge brush

INSTRUCTIONS:
Prep: Using sponge brush, apply Black paint to foam soccer stamp. Stamp on White foam sheet, repeating 6 times. Let dry. Cut out soccer balls leaving a thin line around each ball.
Coozie: Stick 4 balls to coozie. Add words with White foam paint.
Cupcake Marker: Peel backing from 2 remaining balls, place 2 toothpicks in the middle and sandwich soccer balls together. Rub-on player number.

Foam and Glitter 13

1. Color inside outline stickers with Jelly Roll pens.

Stained Glass Cross

Create a beautiful stained glass effect with this simple technique. For a different look, remove the stickers after coloring.

SIZE: 7" x 9½"

MATERIALS:
White foam magnetic cross • *Sakura* (Silver outline stickers, Jelly Roll pens: Teal, Blue, Purple)

INSTRUCTIONS:
Apply outline stickers to cross. Color with jelly roll pens.

Rainbow Fish

Sequins transform into sparkling fish scales on this clever project.

SIZE: 3½" x 6½"

MATERIALS:
Teal fish foam shape • Lime sequins • Foam adhesive

INSTRUCTIONS:
Draw scalloped rows with foam adhesive. Let dry according to package directions. Apply Lime sequins to scalloped adhesive.

1. Lace around wings with chenille stem.

2. Shape Orange stem following pattern.

Butterfly

Add a bit of summer to your room.

SIZE: 5" x 6"

MATERIALS:
Pink foam butterfly shape • Black sticky foam sheet
• Chenille stems (2 Pink, 2 Blue, 2 Orange, 1 Lime Green)
• 2 small wiggle eyes • Green foam marker • Wire cutters
• Round-nose pliers • Push pin • Foam adhesive

INSTRUCTIONS:
Poke holes evenly around outside of butterfly wings. Lace around wings with chenille stems, threading from the bottom to the top. Fold ends down on back of butterfly. • Cut 5" of Green chenille stem, fold in half, swirl ends, and glue to butterfly for antenna. Cut a Black foam body and stick in place. Form butterfly wings with Orange chenille stem following the pattern. To secure shaped Orange stems to butterfly, cut 2 Orange stems 1" long, bend into a "U". Make 2 holes in each side of the butterfly body. Capture the shaped stem under the "U" and push the ends of the "U" through to the back of the butterfly and bend down. Color in a portion of Black body with Green foam marker. Glue on wiggle eyes.

Blue Dolphin

A fun addition to any room.

SIZE: 3" x 7½"

MATERIALS:
Blue Dolphin foam shape • Small wiggle eye • Opal glitter glue • Foam adhesive

INSTRUCTIONS:
Using Opal glitter glue, draw random doodles and squiggles onto dolphin. Let dry. Glue on wiggle eye.

Seahorse

Add some themed sparkle to your room.

SIZE: 3" x 6¾"

MATERIALS:
Teal seahorse foam shape • Small wiggle eye • Glitter glue (Teal, Copper, Purple) • Foam adhesive

INSTRUCTIONS:
Apply glitter glue to seahorse referring to photo. Let dry. Adhere eye.

Finger Puppets
by Kathy Wegner

Create a story with finger puppets. This is a great activity for a scout meeting.

SIZE: 4" x 4"

MATERIALS:
4" x 5" foam (Yellow, Blue, Green, Red) • 4" x 4" foam (Tan, Peach) • 1" x 2" foam (Orange, Black) • 2" x 3" Dark Brown foam • 2½" x 2½" Light Brown foam • Foam markers (Black, Pink, Red) • 3 White 3/8" buttons • Assorted seed beads • White foam paint • Glitter glue • Foam adhesive

1. Adhere hair to face.

2. Decorate body with glitter glue and buttons.

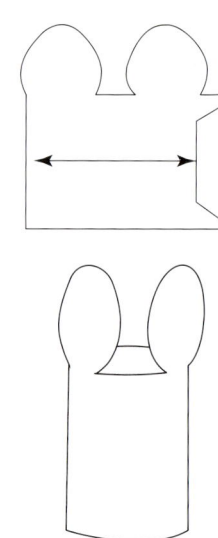

INSTRUCTIONS:
Using patterns, trace designs onto foam and cut out. • Follow Diagram A to glue tabs to form bodies. Glue tops of heads together. See Diagram B.
• Adhere faces, hair, and arms. • Draw facial features with markers. • Decorate bodies with glitter, buttons and beads.

Cardinal Plant Poke
by Kathy Wegner

Cardinals brighten your yard with dazzling color.
SIZE: 3½" x 15"
MATERIALS:
3" x 6" foam (Red, Black) • 12" twig • 2 Black 4mm half round beads for eyes • Foam paint (Black, Gold) • Foam glue
INSTRUCTIONS:
Cut out cardinal pieces from patterns. • Glue twig between both body pieces. Glue 1 wing on each side. Paint entire beak Gold. On both sides, paint face area Black. Let dry. Glue 1 eye bead on each side. Let dry.

Robin Plant Poke

Robins bring Spring... enjoy them all season long.
SIZE: 5" x 13"
MATERIALS:
4" x 6" foam (Brown, Orange) • 12" twig • 2 Black 4mm half round beads for eyes • Foam paint (White, Gold) • Foam glue
INSTRUCTIONS:
Cut out robin pieces from patterns. • Glue twig between both body pieces. Glue 1 breast, 1 wing, and 1 eye bead on each side. Paint entire beak Gold. One both sides, paint neck area above breast White. Let dry.

Dragonfly Plant Poke

Glistening wings add sparkle to your flowers.
SIZE: 5½" x 13"
MATERIALS:
2" x 6" foam (White, Turquoise) • 12" twig • Glitter glue (Opal, Turquoise) • Foam glue
INSTRUCTIONS:
Cut out dragonfly pieces from patterns. • Glue twig between wings and body. Add sparkle to wings and body with glitter glue.

Ladybug Plant Poke

Ladybugs are a welcome guest in any garden.
SIZE: 2½" x 13"
MATERIALS:
2½" x 2½" foam (Red, Black) • 12" twig • Black foam marker • Black foam paint • Foam glue
INSTRUCTIONS:
Cut out ladybug pieces from patterns. Draw center line on Red body. • Glue twig between top and bottom layers. Add spots with Black paint.

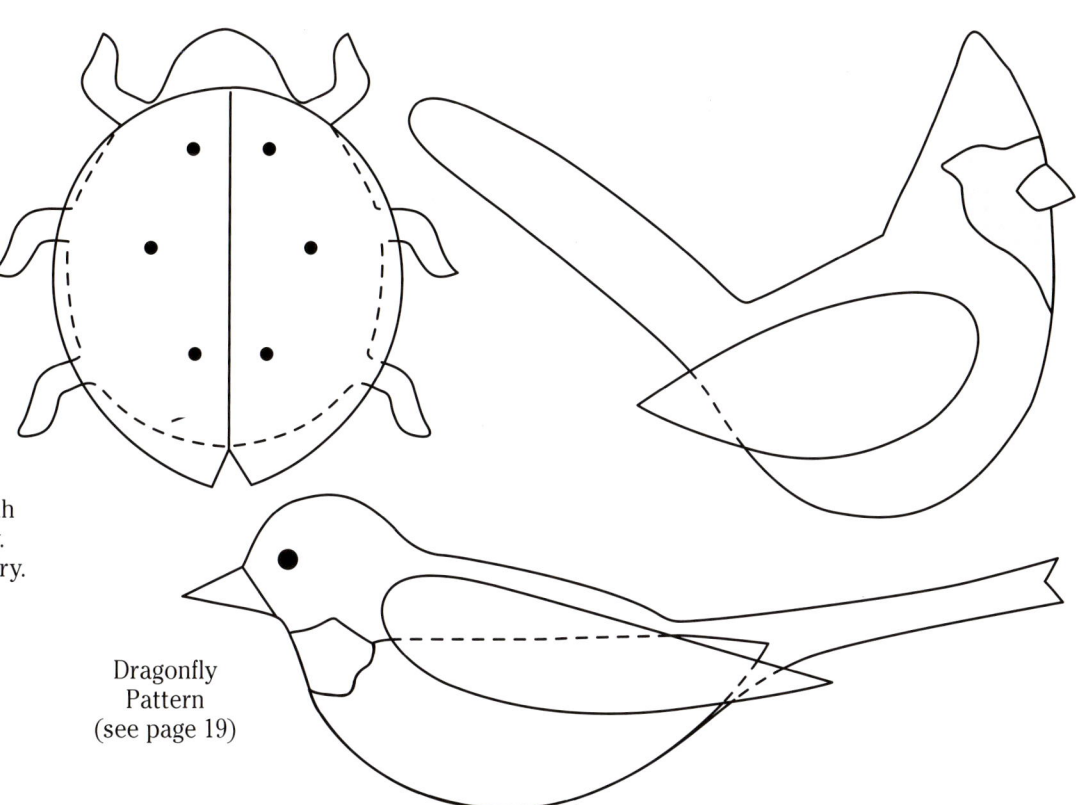

Dragonfly Pattern (see page 19)

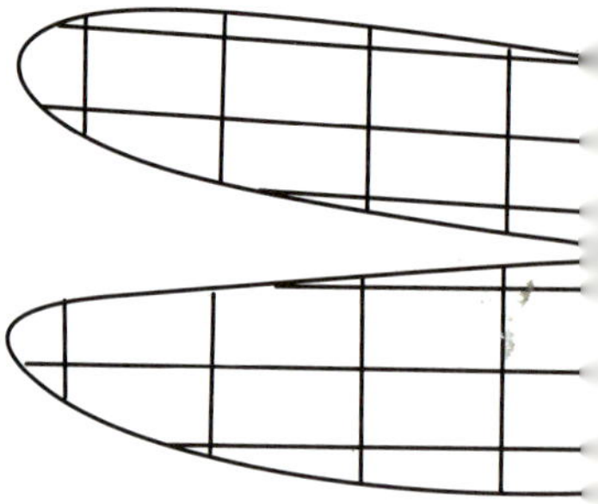

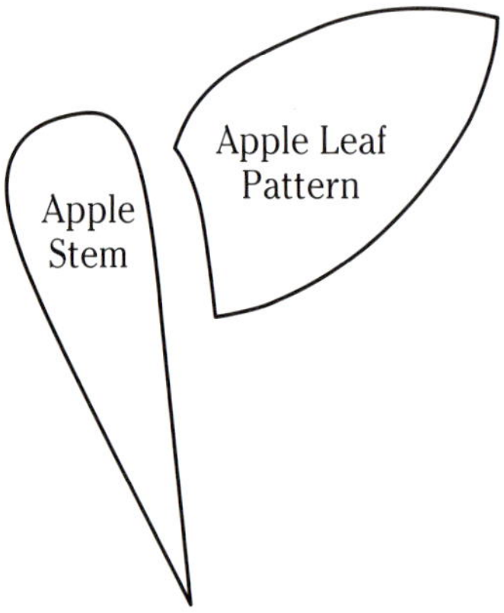

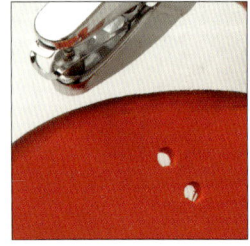
1. Punch 2 holes in the apple.

2. Push ends of ribbon through holes.

3. Tie pencil to apple with ribbon.

'#1 Teacher' Note Pad and Pencil

What a fabulous gift for Teacher Appreciation Day!

SIZE: 5½" x 6"

MATERIALS:
Red Apple foam shape • Sticky foam sheets (Green, Brown) • 12" ruler ribbon ⅝" wide • Pencil • Star-shaped Post-It notes • Green glitter glue • *Clearsnap* Chestnut Roan chalk ink • Crop-A-Dile punch • Paper towel • Foam adhesive

INSTRUCTIONS:
Ink edges of Red foam apple. Dab a paper towel around the edge to soak up excess ink. • Using pattern provided, cut 2 Brown stems and 2 Green leaves from sticky foam sheets and stick onto apple. • Punch 2 holes as shown in photo. From the back, thread ribbon ends through holes and tie pencil in place. • Glue Star Post-it note onto front of apple and write "#1 Teacher" on the first page. Cover Green foam leaf with Green glitter glue, Let dry.

Critter Bucket

Ladybugs, Flowers, and Frogs, Oh my! Here's a fun project that is quick and easy.

SIZE: 1½" diameter, 3" tall

MATERIALS:
Sticky foam shapes (Green frogs, Red ladybugs, Blue and Green flowers) • 5 toothpicks • 1½" bottom diameter Silver bucket • Green decorative grass

INSTRUCTIONS:
Adhere flowers to bucket. • Sandwich toothpicks between matching foam ladybugs and frogs. Fill bucket with decorative grass. Poke toothpicks into grass.

1. Sandwich toothpick between ladybug shapes.

2. Poke toothpicks into grass.